My Spurgeon Souvenirs

A BIOGRAPHY OF C.H. SPURGEON BASED ON SOME MEMORABILIA

ERIC HAYDEN

AMBASSADOR
Belfast • Greenville

My Spurgeon Souvenirs
© 1996 Eric Hayden

First published September 1996

Printed in Northern Ireland

ISBN   1   898787   75   1

AMBASSADOR PRODUCTIONS LTD,
Providence House
16 Hillview Avenue,
Belfast, BT5 6JR

Emerald House,
1 Chick Springs Road, Suite 206,
Greenville,
South Carolina 29609

LIST OF
Contents

ILLUSTRATIONS

INTRODUCTION
Souvenirs or Mementoes?

As a boy I was never into stamp collecting. Soaking labels off match boxes never grabbed me either. Although I was a country boy chasing butterflies with a net was not my cup of tea. I always brought some shells back from the sea-side holidays but neither that nor pressing flowers really fascinated me.

What did interest me, however, being brought up in a Spurgeonic home (CHS framed on the wall, book shelves filled with *The Metropolitan Tabernacle Pulpit* and *The Sword and the Trowel*, not to mention the other works of such a prolific author), was the white marble paper weight, the cartoon pictures, the collection of sermon notes, various etchings and other memorabilia connected with the famous Victorian preacher, his Tabernacle and other institutions.

Were they souvenirs or mementoes? Is there any difference? According to the Oxford Dictionary there is a significant difference. A souvenir is a "thing given or kept in memory of a person or place or event". A memento is "an object kept or serving as a memorial or keepsake". Very little difference? The dictionary adds that a souvenir originated with the Great War (1914-18) and was something demanded by French children from the allied soldiers.

So what may have begun as my grandfather' and father's mementoes, that is, tangible reminders of the Pastor under whose ministry my grandfather sat for many years, and whose children's Orphanage he served in for over fifty years, and the man whom my father grew to love after being taken to his funeral when a mere boy of twelve, these mementoes became his souvenirs. I do not mean that he "demanded" them as the dictionary suggests, nor did I demand them a generation later. But both of us were delighted and proud to inherit them upon the death of the previous owner.

I was the envy of many when I went as a theological student to Spurgeon's College, for I took one or two of these souvenirs to grace my room with. Later, on various preaching engagements and when I ultimately went to the Metropolitan Tabernacle as Pastor, I was given several other objects connected with the great preacher to add to my collection. Some were given to me personally, others were for the new Heritage Room which I started in the newly-built third Tabernacle.

Only recently have I discovered that my souvenirs match up with the various epochs in the life and ministry of Charles Haddon Spurgeon, from his conversion and baptism to his death and funeral.

Unfortunately my collection is far short of what it was almost a decade ago. In 1986 my son was diagnosed as having inoperable cancer and was given three months to live. God granted him a remission for nearly five years, but towards the end of that time he had to give up being pastor of a church and so had to move out of the manse. Many churches and individuals gave very generous gifts towards another residence and my wife and I decided that we too must do all we could. The only way we could make any significant contribution was by selling some of my precious souvenirs. Since, as they say in America: "You British buried Spurgeon but we keep him alive", it seemed that Spurgeon-lovers in America would be the best buyers. With reluctance we sold several, but with rejoicing we were able to give a substantial (for us) gift to our son. In God's plan for our son he never lived in the new house but was called Home to one of the "many mansions" prepared for him by the Lord he had so faithfully served.

Thus it is that I write about some souvenirs that I no longer possess, whereas others still grace the walls and bookshelves of my study. Please, however, do not think that I worship Spurgeon. I worship Spurgeon's God. Neither do I hero-worship Spurgeon, my Saviour is the One who must have the pre-eminence in all things. Spurgeon was, after all, not only a prominent Baptist preacher but also a famous Victorian philanthropist. Some of his institutions are alive and well today; his sermons are still being published, translated, read and preached today; he is still an inspiration to many to undertake preaching the gospel and pastoral charge, and if my humble souvenirs and their history help to further the extension of God's kingdom, then I do not mind in the least being accused of hero-worship.

Souvenirs do not mean a shrine any more than mementoes mean a mausoleum. What souvenirs can do is to remind us of a great Scriptural principle, that God frequently raises up a man, or a woman, for a particular time. Just as secular history has been called "the history of great men", so the history of the Christian Church often centred around God's "man for the hour". From the early days of the Church, from Peter and Paul, to the early Fathers, Clement, Chrysostom and many others, through to Wesley and Whitefield, Moody and Spurgeon, God has raised up special servants for significant service that His Church might know periods of staggering growth and expansion.

hen C. H. Spurgeon was only six years of age, he went into the village alehouse, where one of the members of his grandfather's church was drinking with persons of doubtful character.

He went up to the big man, and astonished him by asking, "What doest thou here, Elijah?" The seasonable rebuke was made a permanent blessing to the man.

~ C.H. Spurgeon Anecdotes

CHAPTER ONE
The Paperback ~ Conversion

The 'spare room' in my parents' home served as a guest room, my father's den, and eventually my bedroom when I was too old to share my brother's room. It had an almost life-size etching of Charles Haddon Spurgeon on the wall. Looking at me over the top of his metal-rimmed glasses prevented me from going to sleep, so I turned him to face the wall.

All round the room were bookshelves housing an almost complete set of Spurgeon's sermons, *The Metropolitan Tabernacle Pulpit*, and several volumes of his monthly magazine, *The Sword and the Trowel*. My interest in the former was merely to look at the pencilled date at the end of many of the sermons, the date on which my grandfather read them at home, having heard it already in the Tabernacle, where, with my grandmother, he was a member.

Lying on top of these volumes in the shelves were many of Spurgeon's other works: single sermons, *Lectures to my Students*, *The Two Wesleys*, *John Ploughman's Talks*, and small pamphlets such as *An Anniversary Speech* (about Dr. Barnardo's Homes) and *A Catechism with Proofs*. Among them was an intriguing paperback called

Spurgeon's Illustrated Almanack, dated 1870. It's subtitle was "Christian's Companion" and it contained "Original Articles by the Editor; texts of Scripture selected for Meditation for every day in the year; Metropolitan Tabernacle Dictionary, etc., etc., (see reproduction of cover on page 11)

By 1870 (the "Almanack" had been started some ten years or so before) the readership was over 60,000. It was an annual production, the daily Bible texts were given on a monthly page. The illustrations were etchings, in the style common in those days, especially in the books like "Pilgrim's Progress", and I suppose that was what fascinated me more than anything.

Besides information relating to the Tabernacle and other Spurgeonic institutions such as the Pastor's College and the Stockwell Orphanage, there were illustrated 'tract-like' articles for believers and unbelievers alike. The one that caught my boyish imagination more than the rest was the father sheltering his small child in his arms during a storm at sea. The helmsman, struggling with the wheel, fired my imagination and impressed on my mind "How to be saved" (the title of that particular page). A reproduction of that message in the "Almanack" is given on page 13.

Spurgeon's salvation experience was a Damascus Road one rather than of a storm at sea. It was sudden, dramatic, and emotional. The storm was a snow storm and this is how he often recounted what happened in 1850 in Artillery Street Chapel, Colchester:

"It was about twenty-six years ago, twenty-six years exactly last Thursday (this was said on Sunday 9 January 1876 - so Spurgeon believed he was converted on the 6th January and not the 13th as some critics would make out!) - that I looked unto the Lord, and found salvation, through this text (Isaiah 45:22). You have often heard me tell how I had been wandering about, seeking rest, and finding none, till a plain, unlettered, lay preacher among the Primitive Methodists stood up in the pulpit, and gave out this passage as his text. He had not much to say, thank God, for that compelled him to keep on repeating his text, and there was nothing needed by me,

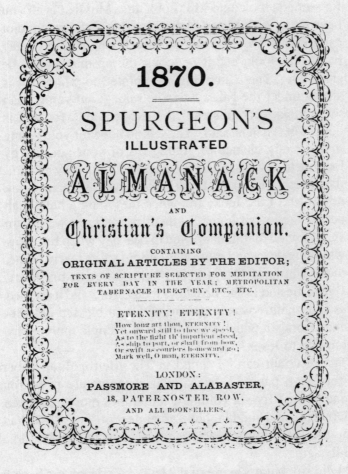

Cover of Spurgeon's Illustrated Almanack

at any rate, - except his text. I remember how he said, "It is Christ that speaks. I am in the garden in an agony, pouring out my soul unto death; I am on the tree, dying for sinners; look unto Me! Look unto Me! that is all you have to do. A child can look. One who is almost an idiot can look. However weak, or however poor, a man may be, he can look; and if he looks, the promise is that he shall live.' Then, stopping, he pointed to where I was sitting under the gallery, and he said, 'That young man there looks very miserable.' I expect I did, for that is how I felt. Then he said, 'There is no hope for you, young man, or any chance of getting rid of your sin, but by looking to Jesus;' and he shouted, as I think only a Primitive Methodist can, 'Look! Look, young man! Look now!' And I did look; and when they sang a hallelujah before they went home, in their own earnest way, I am sure I joined in it. It happened to be a day when the snow was lying deep, and more was falling; so, as I went home, those words of David kept ringing through my heart, 'Wash me and I shall be whiter than snow;' and it seemed as if all nature was in accord with that blessed deliverance from sin which I had found in a single moment by looking to Jesus."

That account can be found in The Metropolitan Tabernacle Pulpit for 1904, page 37, but similar accounts are to be found in every one of the fifty-six volumes, sometimes more than once.

Dramatic and sudden, but a great deal of 'law work' had been done by the Holy Spirit beforehand, as with the apostle Paul. He frequently said:

"I did sin; but my sense of the law of God kept me back from a great many sins ... (the) law had me well in hand";

"I could not find any rest while under the custody of the law ... the law seemed to blight all my hopes ... the law informed me that I was cursed ... there was no rest for my spirit, not even for a moment".

He spoke the above sentences thirty-seven years after his state of conviction, remembering every detail of the spiritual experiences

HOW TO BE SAVED.

THE position of the believer is like that of a child borne upon its father's breast amid a howling tempest. There it rests. There it even sleeps, so perfect is its confidence in the strong arm around it. The force of the wind and the rain fall upon the father, not upon the child. The difficulties of the way may be great, the dangers many, but the child rests calmly and confidently amid them all. This is faith. Christ is all this to me, and to each feeble one who trusts in him. On *his* head the storm *has* fallen ; and now he has pledged his word and his *life* for the safety of those who rest in him. " Because I live, ye shall live also." " They shall never perish, neither shall any man pluck them out of my hand."

Would to God that *you*, my reader, would thus trust him, that this certain salvation and happy confidence might be yours now and henceforth.

Your goodness, moreover, is no recommendation to him, nor your sins any prejudice. Renounce the one as worthless, and boldly bring him the others, that in his *atoning blood* they may be washed away.

O reader, beware, beware ! There is a road to hell hard by the gate of heaven. It is paved with religious observances, crowded with religious people. The Bible is there—formally read. Prayers are there—heartlessly offered ; but surely, certainly, inevitably, yea, as certainly as that broad road of wickedness which you so carefully avoid, does it lead to hell. If you would have life eternal, put no confidence in aught you have done, are doing, or hope to do ; but build your house upon Jesus Christ as upon a solid rock, which nothing in time or eternity can shake, and then all the blessings of the world to come are yours for ever.

Holy works, I need hardly add, will follow, as flowers and fruit follow when a tree is planted in good soil.

Christ first : good works afterward.

that led to his conversion. But it led on into a state of rejoicing and happiness immediately after his conversion experience: on the way home from Artillery Street he wanted to sing and dance with all nature in spite of the deep snow. Arriving home his mother noticed it and said that his "face had changed ... (he) had a smile, a cheerful, happy, contented look ... her melancholy boy had risen out of his despondency and had become bright and cheerful".

Without trying to 'mirror' Spurgeon my own boyish experience was similar. It came about not during a snow storm but during a thunder storm. My mother always shut herself and me in a cupboard beneath the stairs during thunder storms; she was afraid of them. Her fear passed on to me. But at a Crusader camp on the Isle of Wight, as a boy of twelve, I ran across a wide field from my own tent to that of the camp Padre, and told him I wanted to become a Christian. I have not been afraid of thunder ever since!

For months, like Spurgeon, I had been convicted of lying and cheating at home and at school. I had relied on my 'religiosity': church-going three times on a Sunday and various Crusader class meetings during the week. I was intrigued by the change that had come over my elder brother at the previous year's camp and secretly wanted what he had 'got'. That night of the storm my sins were forgiven, I knew I was saved, and I wrote home to my mother telling her how happy I was.

Who knows how much I was influenced by the talk by the camp Padre, or by my mother's prayers, or through the silent but effective Christian witness of my brother? Or was the subconscious influence of the framed photograph of a Victorian preacher I disliked so intensely on the wall of my bedroom? Or may be it was through the influence of his many volumes lining the shelves? Perhaps it was through the small paperback, his "Almanack" containing the simple though powerful message of shelter and salvation by a father during a storm at sea! Only eternity will tell, but in the meantime I treasure the souvenir of the thirty-two page paperback entitled *Spurgeon's Illustrated Almanack and Christian's Companion*, dog-eared and dirty that it has become with the passing of time since 1870.

CHAPTER TWO
The Paperweight ~ Baptsim

Many of the loose Spurgeon sermons, pamphlets, photos and other memorabilia in my parents' spare room were kept from blowing about when the window was wide open during the Summer by a marble paperweight.

About two-and-a-half by four inches (7cm x 10 cm) it had a nob to pick it up by that wobbled in its 'cement' setting. As a small boy I could never understand how the nob did not pull out whenever the paperweight was lifted up. Beneath the weight was a piece of stamp paper (no self-adhesive labels or sellotape in those days) with my grandfather's handwriting informing the user that it was a piece of the original marble baptistry in the Tabernacle after it was burned down on Wednesday, 20 April, 1898. The cause of the fire was probably the over-heating of a flue at one end of the upper gallery. Church records, the communion plate, deeds, paintings and books were saved.

Although the building, known as "The Temple of Nonconformity", had stood since the opening sermon was preached by C. H. Spurgeon on Monday 25 March 1861, was gutted and only the well-known London landmark, the pillared portico left standing, the baptistry was cut into suitable pieces and sold in order to raise funds for the re-building.

The baptistry in the Tabernacle was in a very conspicuous place, immediately beneath the pulpit in the centre of the lower platform. Spurgeon believed in an open, uncovered baptistry, so its white marble was quite an artistic and architectural feature. There were two 'dry wells' in which deacons stood to cover up the candidates with large towels as they emerged from the water.

During Spurgeon's ministry 14,692 people joined the membership of the Tabernacle. Some of these were transferred from other Baptist churches, but the majority were baptised in the marble baptistry by Spurgeon or his associate ministers.

The lower platform was sometimes covered over with boards, especially for midweek meetings such as the prayer meeting. On it were placed over twenty chairs for the elders. Spurgeon used to say that if the boards gave way then his elders would all be baptised by immersion once more!

His own baptism was not in a marble baptistry but in the River Lark in Cambridgeshire. It was some months after his conversion in Colchester and is described in the following words in the first volume of his *Autobiography*, complied after his death by his widow and private secretary:

"To me there seemed to be a great concourse on that weekday. Dressed, I believe, in a jacket with a boy's turn-down collar, I attended the service previous to the ordinance; but all remembrance of it has gone from me: my thoughts were in the water, sometimes with my Lord in joy sometimes with myself in trembling awe at making so public a confession. There were first to be baptised two women - Diana Wilkinson and Eunice Fuller - and I was asked to conduct them through the water to the minister; but this I most timidly declined. It was a new experience for me, never having seen a baptism before, and I was afraid of making some mistake. The wind blew down the river with cutting blast as my turn came to wade into the flood; but after I had walked a few steps and noted the people on the ferry boat and in boats on either shore, I felt as if heaven and earth and hell might all gaze upon

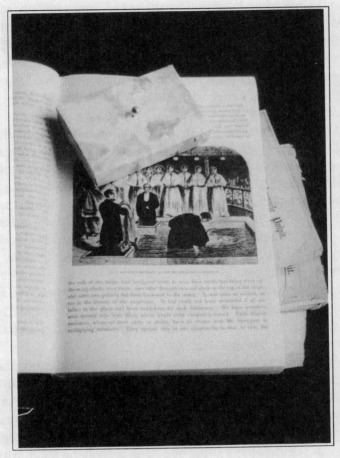

Grandfather's marble paperweight resting on an artist's impression of the young Spurgeon baptising in the baptistry of the Metropolitan Tabernacle. Beneath: original, single printed sermons.

me, for I was not ashamed, there and then to own myself a follower of the Lamb. My timidity was washed away; it floated down the river into the sea and must have been devoured by the fishes, for I have never felt anything of the kind since. I lost a thousand fears in that River Lark and found that 'in keeping His commandments there is great reward'. Baptism also loosed my tongue and from that day it has never been quiet. It was a thrice-happy day to me."

My own profession of Christ as Saviour and Lord should have taken place at the age of sixteen, four years after my conversion. Because my parents thought it would be 'nice' to be baptised with my elder brother I waited another two years. He did not see the Scriptural truth of the believer's baptism by immersion as soon after conversion as I did. I always regret that I waited and did not act in obedience when the Spirit spoke to me. Ever afterwards, in the Baptist ministry, I have tried to encourage young converts not to delay about baptism any more than delay about salvation.

Spurgeon was later to baptise Susannah Thompson (the sweetheart who became his wife), and then his twin sons, Tom and Charles. It was also my privilege to baptise the girl who later became my wife, and then my son and daughter.

Various factors brought me to a decision regarding baptism. It was certainly not seeing other young people in my home church going through the waters of baptism. In fact the first baptism by immersion I ever witnessed was at a Brethren Assembly to which one of my Crusader Class leaders took me and other members of his group. Neither was it through my Bible or a book loaned me about baptism. It could only have been the influence of the Spurgeon literature in my parents' spare room and the marble paperweight that I lovingly fingered and later fondly treasured in remembrance of my Godly grandfather. The marble paperweight softened my stony heart regarding obedience to my Saviour's command. There came the day when I had to yield and say with the hymnwriter: "This the way the Saviour went, Should not the servant tread it still"?

CHAPTER THREE

A Picture Postcard – First Sermon

Beneath the paperweight on my father's desk in the spare room, among the several papers, pamphlets, sermons and tracts, was a faded sepia picture post card. It did not say "Post Card" in English on the reverse, but "Carte Postale" and "Postkarte". Whether it was sent to England from France or Germany I never knew for there is no postmark or stamp on it. It must have come enclosed in an envelope. Whether it was addressed to my father or whether he found it in a book, I never knew.

It is a picture of the cottage at Teversham, Cambridgeshire, where Spurgeon preached his first sermon. On the reverse, in longhand, it is the account of that rather bizarre occasion. (See picture of cottage on page 22)

Spurgeon's first sermon was not his first public address. At Newmarket and Cambridge, and in other places in the Fens, he had had opportunities for "speaking the gospel" in his Sunday school activities. However, in Cambridge there was a Preachers' Association connected with St. Andrew's Street Baptist Chapel. The members supplied the pulpits in the country chapels around Cambridge.

The organising secretary was Mr. James Vinter, known as 'Bishop' Vinter. One day he asked the young Spurgeon to accompany a young man who was rather inexperienced in preaching and conducting services to the village of Treversham. The young man, said the 'Bishop', would be glad of company on his lonely country walk. The story continues in Spurgeon's own words as recorded in the first volume of his *Autobiography*:

> "My Sunday-school work was over, tea had been taken, and I set off through Barnwell, and away along the Newmarket Road, with a gentleman some few years my senior. We talked of good things, and at last I expressed my hope that he would feel the presence of God while preaching. He seemed to start, and assured me that he had never preached in his life, and could not attempt such a thing; he was looking to his young friend, Mr. Spurgeon, for that. This was a new view of the situation, and I could only reply that I was no minister; and that, even if I had been, I was quite unprepared. My companion only repeated that he, in a still more emphatic sense, was not a preacher, that *he* would help me in any other part of the service, but that there would be no sermon unless I delivered one. He told *me* that, if I repeated on of my Sunday-school addresses, it would just suit the poor people, and would probably give them more satisfaction than the studied sermon of a learned divine. I felt that I was fairly committed to do my best. I walked along quietly, lifting up my soul to God, and it seemed to me that I could surely tell a few poor cottagers of the sweetness and love of Jesus, for I felt them in my own soul. Praying for Divine help, I resolved to make the attempt. My text should be, "Unto you therefore which believe He is precious," and I would trust the Lord to open my mouth in honour of His dear Son. It seemed a great risk and a serious trial; but depending upon the power of the Holy Ghost, I would at least tell out the story of the cross, and not allow the people to go home without a word.

We entered the low-pitched room of the thatched cottage, where a few simple minded farm labourers and their wives were gathered together; we sang, and prayed, and read the Scriptures, and then came my first sermon. How long, or how short it was, I cannot now remember. It was not half such a task as I had feared it would be, but I was glad to see my way to a fair conclusion, and to the giving out of the last hymn. To my own delight, I had not broken down, nor stopped short in the middle, nor been destitute of ideas and the desired haven was in view. I made a finish and took up the hymn book; but, to my astonishment an aged voice cried out, "Bless your dear heart, how old are you?" My very solemn reply was, "You must wait till the service is over before making any such enquiries. Let us now sing." We did sing, the young preacher pronounced the benediction, and then there began a dialogue which enlarged into a warm, friendly talk, in which everybody appeared to take part. "How old are you?" was the leading question. "I am under sixty," was the reply. "Yes, and under sixteen," was the old lady's rejoiner. "Never mind my age, think of the Lord Jesus and His preciousness," was all that I could say, after promising to come again, if the gentlemen and Cambridge thought me fit to do so. Very great and profound was my awe of "the gentlemen at Cambridge" in those days.

We are not told if he did return to the Teversham cottage, but he did begin to get other preaching engagements in the villages of Cambridgeshire, his messages being very acceptable to those who heard him. It was early days but already he was being foreseen as "the boy preacher of the Fens".

My own early attempts at preaching followed a similar pattern. I had given the occasional paper at the Christian Endeavour Society in my home church. But one day my father asked me to accompany him on one of his Sunday night visits to a Hertfordshire country 'Bethel'. He was stone deaf and my mother thought he was

Teversham Cottage where Spurgeon preached his first sermon.

rather a danger to himself in the lanes, not being able to hear traffic coming from behind. He was also afraid of falling into a ditch when the evenings were dark and the roads were covered with snow or ice.

Thus we went together, having first pulled thick football socks over our shoes to get a grip on the icy roads. The journey was a silent one as it was before the days of small hearing aids and to make him hear I always had to sit up close and shout. He later said that this was good training for me since if he could hear me then the old ladies sitting at the back of the chapel beneath the gallery would hear me! It certainly worked; the only prize I ever earned in my college course was for elocution - I could shout louder than anyone else! It was also useful for open air work in my first pastoral charge, before the invention of portable amplifiers.

At first I took the Bible reading for my father. Later on I acted as chairman. How privileged I felt when he asked me to serve at the communion table. Eventually I took a service solo, my mother and father sitting in the congregation. My father's comment was, "I heard most of it." My mother's was, "You stood as stiff as a ramrod!"

Was it my mother's worry for my deaf father going to preaching engagements alone that caused me to start preaching? Was it my father's wish to have company on the journey and assistance with the service? Was it a call of God to, "Go ... preach" that came through looking at a picture post card that had such a strange and yet thrilling account of a young man of a previous generation who inspired me?

Spurgeon was still a teenager when he preached his first sermon in that country cottage. He was seventeen years of age, I was sixteen. He was beguiled into preaching, I was subconsciously influenced by a picture postcard that illustrated and described his experience of being God's messenger. His message was, "Unto you who believe He is precious"; mine was, "This poor man cried and the Lord heard him and delivered him from all his troubles." And I looked up Spurgeon's sermon on the text in *The Metropolitan Tabernacle Pulpit* and used much of it!

*M*r. Spurgeon was an admirer of a good full beard as a manly appendage. Meeting a brother minister one day who had grown a fine beard since they last met, he said to him, "Well, Brother ____, I am glad to see your face, so much as I can see. You remind me of the Apostle Paul, who told the Ephesians that, *'They should see his face no more!'*"

~ C. H. Spurgeon Anecdotes

CHAPTER FOUR

A Photographic Portrait ~ Early Ministry

Among the papers under the paperweight in my boyhood home was a photograph. The subject looked podgy, pallid and a bit of a lank-haired (and long haired) prig (schoolboy slang in those days) to my youthful eye. He had pouting lips, one hand hooked into a waistcoat buttonhole and the other raised in the air with a podgy forefinger pointing skywards. Yet this was the photo Spurgeon gave to his fiancee! (see page 27).

Other cartoons under the paperweight, collected by my father from such magazines as "Vanity Fair", showed him again and again in this pose, even sitting on a steam engine like it, "the Spurgeon Express" the newspaper entitled it.

On a visit to London with my father I was taken to see the headquarters of the Baptist Union, then in Kingsway. Inside the building, at the foot of a wide staircase, stood an older, more mature Spurgeon (for he was the subject of the portrait photographer), again with the forefinger pointing upwards. When the Baptist Union moved to Didcot they left Spurgeon behind, as they had down at the Downgrade Controversy, and after lying for some time amidst dust and rubble, it was eventually recovered and placed in the grounds of

Spurgeon's College. For the first time since 1905 when the statue was installed in Kingsway, Southampton Row, London, in Baptist Church House, this seven feet tall bronze figure was lifted off its plinth for transportation and installed in its new home and in September 1992 he came home to his College. Since he died in 1892 it was a fitting year to uproot him and re-establish him - the centenary year of his death.

But why the raised forefinger? Was he being dogmatic, laying down the law? It was more of a foreshadowing of the sixties and seventies "one way sign". Having been led to put his trust in Christ for salvation by being urged to "Look unto Me", that was his emphasis from the earliest days of his ministry right through to the end. He was for ever pointing men to Christ, emphasising the one way to heaven, indicating that Jesus was the only way, the truth and the life. Three sermons (Nos. 245,942 and 2938) were preached by Spurgeon on John 8:14.

Outside Baptist Church House, in a niche, was a statue of John Bunyan, finger pointing to the Bible. What a dynamic duo: one pointing to God's Word and the other to God's living Word, the Word made flesh, the Saviour of the world.

Spurgeon was now "the boy preacher of the Fens". His itinerant preaching was not to be for long. In October 1851, just a few months after his first sermon in the cottage at Teversham, he agreed to supply the pulpit for a few weeks. He remained there for two years. He continued his work at day school in order to augment the £45 per year the church was able to pay him. Waterbeach was notorious for its drunkenness and profanity but in a very short while the tiny thatched chapel was crowded, many of the congregation being hardened sinners who were seen to be repenting and accepting the Saviour with tears and strong crying. Spurgeon described his first convert as being like "a diver who had been down to the depth of the sea, and brought up a rare pearl". The finger pointing men and women to Christ, backed up by evangelical preaching, was the means of many people's eternal salvation and gave the impression to many that he had "leaped full-grown into the pulpit."

An early portrait of Spurgeon.

Around this time a fashionable London church that had fallen on hard times were looking for a new pastor. Although boasting a fine building and a membership of over three hundred, the morning service was attended by only about eighty people. They sent a letter to the young preacher and pastor of Waterbeach which was waiting for him on the vestry table. Thinking they had made a mistake Spurgeon replied that perhaps they had meant it for somebody else. A second letter confirmed that he was really meant and he arranged to preach at New Park Street Chapel, Southwark, London on 18th December 1853.

Word went round after the morning service and at night the chapel was well attended. He was the first interrugnum preacher to be invited a second time and he returned for three Sundays in January 1854. An invitation to the pastorate soon followed but Spurgeon would only agree to a trial period of three months. At the end of that period he agreed to become their full time pastor. He was only twenty years of age.

Before leaving Waterbeach he wrote to his grandfather and said, "Souls, souls, souls, I hope this rings in my ears, and hurries me on." It certainly did at New Park Street Chapel. Soon the streets around the chapel were blocked and the congregation overflowed so that many had to listen as best they could from outside. The chapel was enlarged during 1855. During the three months of extension work services were held in the Exeter Hall in the Strand, thus causing the secular press to become even more curious and to produce more 'one finger pointing upwards' caricatures. To the Spurgeon 'Fast Train' or 'Express' was now added 'Brimstone and Treacle' as he was compared with the newspaper idea of a Church of England clergyman. 'Catch-em-alive o'", a representation of Spurgeon attracting the gullible public like a fly-paper, and the Archbishop of Canterbury and Spurgeon as rival bus conductors, these and more were some of the amusing, yet often slanderous, criticisms of one who was merely trying to point people to Jesus.

When pastor and people returned to the enlarged New Park Street Chapel they realised they had wasted their money. The crowds were bigger than ever and once again the Exeter Hall had to be engaged for Sunday evening services. New Park Street Chapel was used for the morning worship.

There was only one thing to be done. A special building, "the largest chapel in the world" must be built for him. A fund was started and because the Exeter Hall was no longer available the Surrey Gardens Music Hall, able to accommodate ten to twelve thousand people, was hired. Enthusiastic crowds filled it, in spite of the fact that a terrible catastrophe occurred one Sunday evening through some 'yobbos' (as we would call them today) crying out "Fire! fire!" This resulted in even more criticism and cartoon drawings.

Now the 'smart set', society and aristocracy, Members of Parliament, royalty and other prominent people were to be seen in his congregation. He was back in the Music Hall and the services continued there for another three years, even though the national newspapers were describing it as "grotesque as a gargoyle."

The preacher's index finger pointed heavenwards; the finger of history points to a little thatched Cambridgeshire chapel and then to a south London fashionable chapel in dire need of a fresh injection of the doctrines of grace.

Once again my own experience of ministry began in a similar way. During my college course after World War II, at Spurgeon's College, London, I was allowed to go to a "student pastorate". Several of us, as more mature students (having served in the Forces during the war), were allowed to give pastoral oversight to some small church while continuing our theological studies. I was invited to a very small village chapel (not with a thatched roof!) where I preached twice or three times a month and spent a certain amount of time in pastoral visitation. Some weekends I would take a team of students from the college with me and on the Saturday night we would hold an evangelistic rally. Soon there were conversions and the baptistry opened once again after being closed for about fifteen years!

People advised me not to accept their invitation as I would 'be buried alive' in the country! It certainly was not so. Even though I did not follow in Spurgeon's footsteps and go immediately to his Metropolitan Tabernacle, I was being prepared for that challenge by going first to a seaside church in the north east of England and then to a county town chapel in the largest inland shire of England. In each place I hope I pointed men, women and young people to Spurgeon's Saviour.

CHAPTER FIVE

Paraphernalia ~ The Tabernacle

J ust as my father and grandfather gathered memorabilia about Spurgeon, which eventually became 'housed' in the spare room, and then in my manse study when I entered the ministry, so I began to collect my own paraphernalia. Paraphernalia was the word used by relatives and friends, perhaps by some in a derogatory sense. The dictionary defines the word as "personal belongings or accessories, odds and ends of equipment". I have handled several items of Spurgeon's personal belongings in both the college and the Tabernacle heritage room: his spectacles, walking stick, shirt collar (detached, no such thing as an all-in shirt in those days!), and even a test tube filled with some of his and Susannah's wedding cake! My paraphernalia was of a different kind; most of it has to do with his Metropolitan Tabernacle.

First there came into my possession, at a price, one of the original Tabernacle communion plates. When the second Tabernacle was destroyed by enemy bombs during the Second World War, there was no marble baptistry to sell off as paperweights to gather funds for the third Tabernacle. The deacons instructed me, however, to sell off the twenty communion plates to a London jeweller. With hindsight it would have been better advertising them over in America for Spurgeon-lovers they would have paid a better price! I obtained £9 per plate and one of them at that price for myself (see page 33).

I used to love, as a boy, hearing my grandfather describe a Tabernacle communion service, with twenty-nine elders breaking up the loaves on to the plates for distribution to the believers in the congregation. The believers were asked to sit in the floor area and the first gallery; spectators were consigned to the second gallery, and time and again Spurgeon heard of those who were converted in the upper gallery through watching the communion service below. Sometimes he would look up to the second gallery and addressed a few words to the spectators. In his magazine *The Sword and The Trowel* for 1880 he recorded among his monthly "Personal Notes" the case of an old Christian man who had come up from the country to hear Spurgeon. As a spectator at the Lord's Table some words of the preacher convicted him and he was converted and went home to be baptised and join the church.

Spurgeon believed in a weekly observance of Communion and even when recuperating from illness at Menton in the South of France he would gather a few friends for communion in his hotel room. His meditations before observing the ordinance on those occasions are choice and have been gathered together in book form. A sermon on "The Object of the Lord's Supper" given at the Tabernacle on 2 September, 1877 is to be recommended. It was published after his death and is to be found in the 1905 volume of *The Metropolitan Tabernacle Pulpit* (volume 51).

Cups and saucers from the old Tabernacle days of huge tea meetings' were also sold for rebuilding funds. Many of them were chipped or racked, but I managed to find one in very good condition (see page 34). Rather than being hidden away in my study it has always taken pride of place in the centre of our Welsh dresser. It is sometimes a good talking point that leads to higher things.

Originally the cups and saucers were fired for fund-raising in 1861 so that the Tabernacle could be opened free from debt. It is interesting to note that the reproduced photograph on page 34 was one of a portfolio of mine when I was upgraded from ASAI

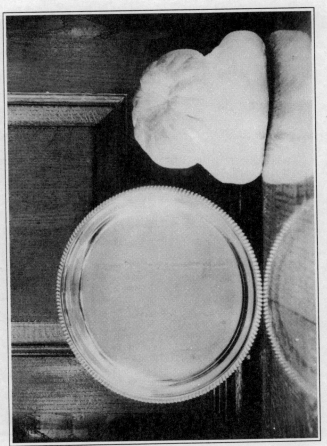

One of the original Tabernacle communion plates.

A Tabernacle cup and saucer.

(Associate of the Society of Architectural Illustrators) to MSAI (Membership). It was included in my section of illustrations of "architecture in unusual forms" (1978).

A third Tabernacle souvenir was a 'find' in a second hand junk shop. It cost the princely sum of ten shillings (50 pence metric money). A 'princely' sum since I was a poor theological student at the time. It was a seven-and-a-half inches (20 cms) high bust or statuette of Spurgeon. They were cast in 1878, Spurgeon's "Testimonial Year", and were sold to raise funds for erecting the Almshouses. Over $5,000 was necessary and that figure was surpassed through the generosity of well wishers. (See page 36)

The sculptor was John Adams-Acton, a gold medallist of the Royal Academy. He had already provided the bust of John Wesley for Westminster Abbey, and also one of Queen Victoria for the Bahamas.

The same bust of Spurgeon, in various heights, replicas of the original are to be found in many church vestries and minister's manses in England and in other parts of the world.

They were on sale to Tabernacle members and friends in the year when the membership of the church stood at 5,040 and in a building that seated 6,000 the preacher sometimes had to ask his regular congregation to stay away some Sunday evenings so that the building could be filled with strangers to the gospel. In May of that "Testimonial Year" such a call went out and the building was filled with unbelievers who heard a sermon entitled "No Difference" (No. 1414), the text being, "He maketh his sun to rise on the evil and on the good, and sendeth rain on the just and on the unjust" (Matthew 6.45).

Thus the Tabernacle ministry began, continued and ended with the Prince of Preacher's death in 1892. It began with the foundation-stone laying by Sir Samuel Morton Peto., Bart., MP on 18 August, 1859. The entire structure was 174 feet long complete with ancillary rooms. The chapel itself was 146 feet long by 81 feet wide and was built ten feet above ground so that half-basement Sunday school rooms and lecture halls could be built underneath. The seating capacity was 5,000 with an added 1,000 flaps that could be let down at the end of the pews. It was opened in March 1961 at a total cost of £31,000. For

Statuette of Spurgeon cast in 1878.

thirty-one years C. H. Spurgeon proclaimed the doctrines of grace in this mammoth building with 150 new members being received into fellowship at one communion service and in one record year (1872). 571 new members were added to the church. If members had not moved to other districts or emigrated the building would have been totally inadequate. The greatest crowds to be seen in the building were on the 8 February, 1892 when the body of Spurgeon lay in state. A procession of 60,000 people passed by to view the coffin. On the 10th of that month the building was filled four times over for the funeral sermon.

My own call to the pastorate of the Tabernacle came some time after I had written an article for *The Sword and the Trowel* entitled "Pew 49" the seat in which my grandparents sat.

It was a difficult five years and they can be read about in *The Sword and the Trowel*, volumes 1956-61. That period is summed up in *A Centennial History of Spurgeon's Tabernacle*. Briefly it can be summarised: the third Tabernacle was opened like the two previous ones, free from debt; fifty nine new members were added to the church during the first two years, and one hundred had been baptised by the end of the pastorate. In the light of Spurgeon's statistics these figures seem but a drop in the bucket, but there has only been one Spurgeon. Churches may hope and pray that there minister will be another CHS but Charles Haddon Spurgeon was God's man for the times in which he lived. Not even his gifted son Thomas could fill the Tabernacle as his father had when he succeeded him to the pastorate.

During my Tabernacle pastorate a personal tragedy occurred. In my grandfather's Tabernacle hymn book in which he had written his name and pew number (see page 38) he had pencilled in against the verse of a hymn ("Ten thousand times ten thousand") the names of one daughter and two sons who had predeceased him. Besides my father and two other sons who had done well in life (one a police inspector and the other on the stock exchange) there was a son who had become a vagrant or a 'gentleman of the road'. No one in the family had heard from him for many years.

One day a policeman knocked at the door of the manse and told us (my father was then a widower and living with us) that this

Portrait of the Author's grandfather, taken by him at the age of 16.
Below the portrait the inscription in his Tabernacle hymn book denoting
his pew number.

long lost brother of his had been found seriously ill in a lodging house near the Tabernacle. They had taken him to hospital.

I visited him several times, always reading some Scripture verses to him and praying with him. When I introduced myself to him and told him I was the pastor of the near-by Tabernacle, he said he knew that. I believe he died trusting Christ, but what a waste of a life, especially after being bought up in the Tabernacle Sunday school and siting under evangelical ministry Sunday by Sunday. He had also been in a home where the Spurgeonalia or memorabilia had been much in evidence. We can only enter into the joyous truth of the hymn marked in the Pew 49 hymn book:

> *O then what raptured greetings*
> *On Canaan's happy shore.*
> *What knitting severed friendships up,*
> *Where partings are no more!*
>
> *Then eyes with joy shall sparkle*
> *That brimmed with tears of late;*
> *Orphans no longer fatherless,*
> *Nor widows desolate.*

Twenty seven years later I was to add the name 'Philip' beneath my grandfather's sons in his hymn book. My only son died of cancer at the age of 34.

At a meeting of the Board of Trustees of the Stockwell Orphanage, one day, when the business was concluded, Mr. Spurgeon said in a very grave and solemn tone, "Before we separate, I have a most serious matter to bring before you. It has to do with the Head Master, Mr. Charlesworth. He has introduced a child into the Orphanage without the consent of any of the Trustees."

The Trustees were astonished, and all looked very grave. Questions were asked, great surprise was expressed, and they were proceeding to discuss the Master's conduct, when Mr. Spurgeon's gravity began to give way, and it soon came to the remembrance of some of them that Mrs. Charlesworth had recently presented her husband with a son.

~ C. H. Spurgeon Anecdotes

CHAPTER SIX

A Presentation – The Orphanage

A mong the plethora of biographies of C. H. Spurgeon that appeared soon after his death in 1892 the one liked best in our spare room 'library' was that by J. C. Carlile, CH. This was not because of better factual information, nor higher literary merit, but simply for sentimental reasons. This "Interpretative Biography" was a presentation to my grandfather after he had served for 54 years as a joint-superintendent of the Sunday School of Spurgeon's Orphanage Homes. Originally known as Stockwell Orphanage Spurgeon provided for 250 boys and the same number of girls. My grandfather was superintendent of the boys' Sunday school, being appointed to that important and responsible position in 1880, (See presentation flyleaf reproduced on page 42)

When Pastor of the Tabernacle I searched in vain for a record of the date he joined the Tabernacle membership. All I know is that he bought several of Spurgeon's literary works as they appeared and the earliest one is dated 1879. It is hard to believe that he was appointed to such a prominent position after only being in membership for twelve months. Even so, if that was the correct date then he must have 'sat under' Spurgeon for 13-14 years.

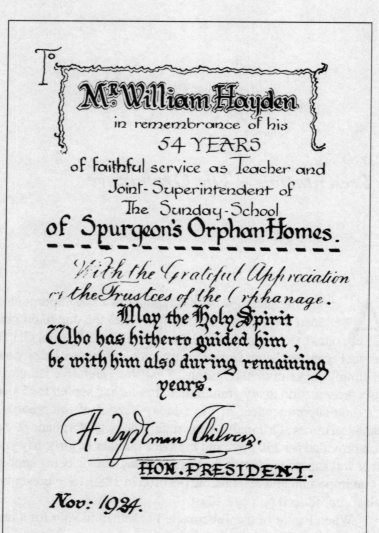

To

Mr William Hayden
in remembrance of his
54 YEARS
of faithful service as Teacher and
Joint-Superintendent of
The Sunday-School
of Spurgeon's Orphan Homes.

With the Grateful Appreciation
of the Trustees of the Orphanage.
May the Holy Spirit
Who has hitherto guided him,
be with him also during remaining
years.

A. Tydeman Chilvers.
HON. PRESIDENT.

Nov: 1924.

Facsimile of inscription in book presented to Author's grandfather.

As a small boy I could not say that I had much appreciation of his service for the Stockwell Orphanage, and even less appreciation of the orphans themselves. Whenever we went to stay with him he would take out of the kitchen dresser a huge bag of sweets every Sunday after dinner. I was never allowed one of them for "these are for my orphans". I began to dislike those orphans and envied them their Sunday treat! As I got older I understood what he was doing and something of his love for the orphan boys.

Some years later, when my parents took me to the seaside for our summer holiday, we would visit the orphans who were also on holiday and had several beach huts in a row in which to change for bathing and in which to shelter if it should rain. Playing with them I began to understand something of their life in "Spurgeon's Homes" (as it was then called) and realised they fully deserved those Sunday sweets.

Spurgeon described the inception of the Orphanage in a sermon in 1884 in these words:

"It is striking to see, as you and I see, a woman of moderate wealth discarded all the comforts of life in order to save sufficient funds to start an orphanage in which the children might be cared for, not merely, as she said, for the children's sake, but for Christ's sake, that He might be glorified."

Through reading his magazine, *The Sword and the Trowel*, Mrs. Anne Hillyard became the benefactor to so many children. She wrote to the editor, C. H. Spurgeon, offering £20,000 for the founding and erection of an orphanage for fatherless children. Spurgeon had already challenged his Monday night prayer meeting with the words, "We are a huge church, and should be doing more for the Lord in this great city. I want us tonight to ask Him to send us **some new work**; and if we need money to carry it on, let us pray that **the money may also be sent.**"

Contributions large and small soon flowed in, but it was Mrs. Hillyard's generous contribution that was God's seal upon the scheme. Brought up in the Plymouth Brethren she later married a Church of England clergyman. As a widow she saw how a long-cherished idea and dream might be fulfilled. When Spurgeon received the cheque he queried the number of noughts on the amount with Mrs. Hillyard, thinking she had written too many!

My favourite biographer described the building as "a box or barrack like erection". The children were placed in 'houses' and each house had its own 'mother' or matron. A spacious hall was built for religious services and other meetings, and it was here my grandfather superintended the vast Sunday school.

The first building was for boys but soon a girls' wing was added, once more Anne Hillyard being the first subscriber. There was a sick bay, gymnasium, swimming pool, dining hall and outside beautiful lawns, flower beds, trees and shrubs. It now had the overall impression of a park rather than an institution.

Neither was it institutional in the sense of dress or uniform. They dressed as other children so that they were not stigmatised in the streets. On Sundays they went to the services at the Tabernacle forming what Spurgeon called 'his choir'. He often visited the Orphanage and the children loved him. When unable to go because of illness he wrote them letters instead.

During World War II and the 'blitz' on London the Orphanage was evacuated to Godalming in Surrey. Property was then purchased in Reigate.

When war ended new Spurgeon's Homes were built at Birchington, Kent. I had the privilege of laying a foundation stone for the Homes' Chapel at Birchington, on behalf of the Tabernacle. I wondered at the time what grandfather was thinking. Little did I dream of having such a connection with the orphanage when I used to read and finger the presentation 'address' in the front of Carlile's biography and though of how I was envious of the children partaking of grandfather's sweets.

In the '70s and '80s it was seen that the orphanage method of caring for children was not dealing with the sufferings of children from broken homes. The Birchington buildings were sold and the children sent to different parts of the country and placed in more flexible units. Now they are housed in centres like Coventry, Wolverhampton and Bedford, the emphasis being on family day care, fostering, adoption, preventative treatment and hostel accommodation. Grandfather would have a hard task distributing his bag of sweets now, and an even harder job superintending a Sunday school! I'm sure however, he would have approved of anything that enhanced their lot in life, and he would rejoice that Spurgeon's Child Care still stresses the Christian message as being imperative for the restoration and renewal of family life.

*A*ddressing his students one day, Mr. Spurgeon said, "If you should attempt the grand in your preaching, mind you are sure of not making a fool of yourself, as the Brother did who exclaimed, "It thundered, brethren - it thundered like ... like ... like ... anything.' Nor yet he who, describing the angels ascending and descending Jacob's ladder, said, "They went up and down like ... like ... like ..." but he did not know what to liken their movements to, but only made himself look like a fool."

~ C. H. Spurgeon Anecdotes

CHAPTER SEVEN

Pastoralia ~ The College

Among the books by Spurgeon in my parent's spare room-cum-father's den-cum-my bedroom, I discovered one that greatly helped me when I began to preach at the age of sixteen in the Hertfordshire village chapels. "Healthy, happy, hearty Hertfordshire" Charles Lamb called my home country. The villages had names that were like music to my teenage ears as I went round them, first on foot with my father, then on my cycle. London Colney (nothing to do with the London, and not a bit like it), Sandridge. Tyttenhanger, Kings Langley, and so on. Some of them housed the famous such as George Bernard Shaw. Each one had its small village Baptist Church, some the offspring of a mother church in St. Albans, other belonging to the county town, Hertford, and so on. Some had part time lay pastors who perhaps only preached twice a month. Others had no such pastoral oversight at all. A local lay preacher's association arranged the preachers' plan and also organised annual lay preachers' classes.

Helpful as it was to meet with other lay preachers of all ages, and listen to the lectures mainly given by full time Baptist ministers, it was *Lectures to my Students* by C. H. Spurgeon that helped me most.

Somebody once said, "Charles Haddon Spurgeon is the only dead Baptist who is alive - he survives in his institutions!" Of these Spurgeon referred to his College as his "first born and best beloved".

He longed to see young men, converted to Christ, fervent in faith, but mostly untrained in culture, education and theology, being taught the rudiments of preaching and the pastoral office. Thus he placed the apostrophe after the 's' and not before it. It was not to be referred to as the Pastors' College, that is, the pastor of the Tabernacle's college, but the Pastors' College or the college for would-be pastors.

He began with one student, T. W. Medhurst. A member of New Park Street Chapel, he began, after his conversion, to preach in the open air. He had a great measure of success but also many criticisms of his lack of education. Spurgeon sent him to a Baptist Minister at Bexley Heath for personal coaching, and then once a week he studied theology with Spurgeon himself. This one-to-one tutorial was first of all in Spurgeon's bachelor lodgings. After his marriage to Susannah Thompson the student studied in their home.

Soon he was joined by a second student and they went to live with the Rev. George Rogers of Camberwell, a Congregational minister. Some would date the beginning of the pastors' college from that time, 1856. Every month the numbers grew until there were forty. By the time Spurgeon died nine hundred men had been trained in his college.

It was now too large for George Rogers' home so the basement halls of the Tabernacle were first used for lectures, the students being in lodgings with Tabernacle members. After fourteen years the college outgrew the Tabernacle premises and a college building was erected at the back of the Tabernacle in 1874.

From the sale of his books Spurgeon reckoned to spent £600-800 per year on his college men's training. George Rogers became the first recognised Principal.

Each week Spurgeon lectured in the college. The preacher's inner life, his public delivery, elocution, gesticulation, illustration, these and many other facets of the preacher's and pastor's work were dealt with in Spurgeon's lectures. They were published in several volumes, my favourite being *The Art of Illustration*. Country chapels were notorious for being overheated in the winter and the farmers and other outdoor workers had a job not to go to sleep during the sermon. A well chosen and well told illustration was one sure way of keeping interest from flagging.

My father's signed copy is dated 1901 yet the book was published in 1894 after Spurgeon's death. He revised the first two lectures and partially revised three others. The rest were printed from reporters' transcripts. My copy still has the pencil marks in the margins which I made long, long ago. The index is a mine of information for those stuck for an illustration to make a point more palatable in a doctrinal sermon.

So I could go on about the other three volumes, and the second in particular. The two lectures on gesticulation ("Posture, Action, Gesture, etc.") are masterpieces and the engravings brilliantly executed, catching the eye and the imagination of a sixteen year old completely. "The Very Rev. Dr. Paul preaching in London" and "Brimstone and Treacle" (depicting Spurgeon himself) are certainly the best. (See page 50)

As I stuck Dr. Angus' *Bible Handbook* and Spurgeon's *Lectures* in the saddle bag of my cycle and went for a cycle ride into the Hertfordshire countryside on a Saturday afternoon, I never dreamed that many years later I would be a student myself at Spurgeon's College.

After six years army and coal mine service during World War II the time came for my entry into Spurgeon's College. By now it had moved from the rear of the Tabernacle (in 1923) to Falkland Park, South Norwood Hill.

Today it is the largest Baptist College in the British Isles although its links with the Tabernacle have been finally severed.

Before leaving the army I had the sad news that my grandfather was seriously ill and had not got long to live. Being given compassionate leave to visit him I went to the Salvation Army nursing home, situated quite near to the college. Knowing that God had called me to be a preacher, but never had heard me, he said that he would be looking down from the "bulwarks of heaven" to see and hear me

THE VERY REVEREND DR PAUL
PREACHING IN LONDON.

BRIMSTONE   AND   TREACLE.

Engravings from Lectures to My Students.

when I eventually became a Baptist minister. Surely Hebrews 12:1 must have been in his mind - "Wherefore seeing we also are compassed about with so great a cloud of witnesses." I have often thought of him during forty years or so when standing in the pulpit proclaiming the same doctrines of grace he heard from the Prince of Preachers, and he himself believed in most firmly.

CHAPTER EIGHT

Paintings ~ Family Circle

When I was pastor of Spurgeon's Metropolitan Tabernacle I was given two watercolour paintings by a Baptist minister. One was for me to keep and the other was for the church vestry wall. Mine was entitled "In Dartmouth Harbour" and was No. 72 which means it was part of an exhibition. (See page 52 and 53)

The artist was Thomas Spurgeon, twin son of Charles and Susannah Spurgeon. Eighty-seven year ago, in 1909, Thomas held his first exhibition of paintings in a New Bond Street gallery. Out of the 80 pictures hung, 40 were sold! Two years later another exhibition was held and on that occasion 100 paintings were hung. A third showing was held in aid of his father's Stockwell Orphanage, Tom paying for all the framing out of his own pocket so that all profit could go to the orphanage.

It was unprecedented for a Baptist minister to hold such exhibitions in the centre of London, and report has it that his work was also hung at the Royal Academy.

Susannah Thompson and Charles Haddon Spurgeon were married when Spurgeon was still at New Park Street Chapel. From the

"In Dartmouth Harbour"

"Devon Scene"

very beginning, when CHS preached 'with a view' to the pastorate she disliked him.

He appeared country-bumkin in dress, uncouth in speech, and far from the cultured style of ministry the church had been used to with Drs. Rippon and Gill as his two illustrious predecessors. However, things changed, and soon they fell in love, became engaged and were married on 8 January 1856.The honeymoon was spent in Paris. Twin sons were born in September 1856.

Having been forbidden by his mother to take up drawing lessons at school, Thomas began painting while convalescing after an illness later in life. He painted scenes in Tyrol, Bavaria, Italy, Switzerland and in many places in England, especially localities connected with his father's life and ministry. He spent many a relaxing hour in Essex and Cambridgeshire capturing scenes such as Isleham Ferry, scene of his father's baptism; the cottage in which his father preached his first sermon, and so on. When he exhibited *The Baptist Times* later reported that Thomas was "an artist born not made". *The Daily Graphic* wrote that he and "an aptitude for colour and a happy knack of seizing the picturesque."

On leaving school Tom was apprenticed to a wood engraver in Fetter Lane, London. He soon developed lung trouble and it was decided a sea voyage would be the best treatment. He sailed to Australia and on board ship used his artistic talents in the navigation room, drawing charts, sea scenes and a block of the ship he was sailing in. He landed 'down under' with the idea of continuing his work as an engraver, but when the Australians found he could "preach a bit", he spent the time fulfilling an itinerant ministry. Soon an invitation came from New Zealand but he had to return home to take his father's place at the Tabernacle while CHS was ill.

He entered Spurgeon's College but was frequently absent from lectures through illness. Once more he set sail for Australia. Within two years he was in New Zealand and quickly accepted the pastorate of Auckland Baptist Church. He built a new chapel on similar illness to the architecture of his father's London Tabernacle, seating 1,200 people. Once again ill-health struck and he had to resign the pastorate. After an evangelistic career he succeeded his father at the

Tabernacle when C.H. Spurgeon died. The original Tabernacle was burned down and Tom took up the challenge of rebuilding. At the end of 1905 over 700 had confessed Christ but within two years more ill-health resulted in his resignation. He continued to preach for a while but it was mainly drawing and painting and writing that occupied his time. But in October 1917 a pain between the eyes rendered him unconscious and his artist's eyes soon saw no more of God's natural world that he had painted and engraved so diligently and delightfully.

Twin brother Charles had the same upbringing and education but when Tom was apprenticed to an engraver Charles entered a city merchant's office. Like Tom, brother Charles entered the father's college and at the end of his course became pastor of South Street Baptist Chapel, Greenwich, London. Whereas Tom sometimes produced illustrations for *The Sword and the Trowel*, Charles helped his father with book reviews for that magazine.

In 1894, two years after his father's death, Charles resigned his pastoral charge and went to South Africa. He resigned on the grounds of ill-health, never having fully recovered from a severe bout of influenza caught three years previously.

When his health picked up he returned to England and became pastor of Salem Baptist Church, Cheltenham, Gloucestershire, but only for twelve months. His next pastoral charge was Nottingham. Again it was a short one and he was soon inducted as minister of Holland Road Baptist Church, Hove, on the south coast. It was during the difficult days of the First World War but he "stirred everything to new life." Under difficult circumstances. He also became the full time President-Director of his father's Orphanage, an ideal public relations officer for them. He died in December 1926 and it is generally acknowledged that he lived under the shadow of his illustrious father and his twin brother. Although he was more at his father's side while Tom was in Australia, so much publicity was made of Tom's exploits in *The Sword and the Trowel* that it was Tom who was always in the limelight.

As the father's sermons still speak today, through the republishing of the many volumes, so the son's paintings still move hearts to generosity. A lady wrote to me saying that she had two of Tom Spurgeon's water colours which she would sell and give the money to the Home Mission Fund of the Baptist Union. One was of Canterbury and the other a Devonshire scene. Both were numbered on the back as they were exhibited in the Bond Street exhibition. As a result of the sale of Tom's two paintings in recent times some Baptist preacher in a small, struggling cause, was enabled by a grant of money towards his stipend, to do as Tom did and "master his art ... and sharpen his tools". He said in his introduction to his own published sermons, "Down to the Sea" - "I make no apology for introducing illustrations. I confess to a weakness for pictures. I ploughed the boxwood with my graver before I ploughed the seas in a ship. If woodcuts seem to detract from the dignity of a volume of sermons, what matters is they add to its usefulness? This I confidently expect them to do."

My sentiments exactly! After school, having taken art in school, I attended technical college to learn commercial art. Owing to the outbreak of war I thought this would end such training but for nearly a year I was able to attend part time while stationed near a college. The army made good use of me, posters, signs, and especially drawing bombs in difficult places waiting to be defused!

In Spurgeon's College I became "college artist" and in my pastorate I have saved them a great deal of money designing posters and 'fliers' for special occasions but I have found, like Tom Spurgeon, that I could illustrate God's message. Flannelgraph, magnetic board, flash boards, blackboards, flip-boards - these and other kinds of illustrated gospel messages have been successfully used.

When I left college to go to my first pastorate my collage Principal charged me to "draw pictures of Christ" for my congregation. He meant *word* pictures, but the idea behind his saying was that I was to let the artist's imagination have full sway in depicting "Christ and Him crucified". Sometimes I felt alone in those now long-ago days of early ministry, for no one else seemed to be using much visual aid in the pulpit, except for specialised children's evangelists. The discovery of artist Tom Spurgeon later confirmed what I had been doing, and reviews by his illustrious father when recommending books in his monthly magazine. The drawing of blackboard objects to accompany a gospel message he called, "first rate", and "visual" as well as "verbal" methods of teaching Sunday school children should be made "good use of". At last I felt in good company!

A woman in Victoria, Australia wrote to Spurgeon telling of blessing received many years ago. "At that time I lost a darling boy, everything seemed dark and nothing brought me any comfort. A friend brought me one of your sermons. I forget the title of it, but it was that everything is ordered by God, nothing comes by chance. When I had finished it I leaped from my couch, and said, 'All is right; thank God! my dark mind is all light again.'

From that time my husband ordered your sermons monthly, and we continue to do so. Every Sunday evening we read one aloud, so that all may hear, and afterwards I send them into the Bush."

~ C. H. Spurgeon Anecdotes

CHAPTER NINE

Publications - The Written Word

My father always had an evening quiet time sitting in his armchair just as the rest of us were ready for bed. He said the house was nice and quiet then. As he was stone deaf I could not see that that made any difference!

He had had his morning Bible reading on the train going up to London from St. Albans. The rest of the compartment were probably having a card school but he could not hear them. One of the blessings of deafness was the way he looked at it.

In the evening, after his Bible reading I noticed as a small boy that he read from a small red volume. One day he came home from work and proudly showed me how it had been rebound for him. I noticed in the flyleaf that he had had it since 1911, and that his favourite pages were listed in the front. Inside the pages were browned and fraying at the edges through much use. He bought me a similar book when I went into the army but mine was black morocco leather. On the flyleaf he had written Philip Henry's saying, "Never see the face of man until you've seen the face of God." Rather a tall order when the sergeant came round tipping you all in the barrack-room out of bed.

As time went by I began to value the contents of this little book as much as my father had done. So much so that I gave my fiancee a copy two years before we were married, on her birthday. Her and mine were reproductions, my father's was an original, a first edition, published by Passmore and Alabaster of London, the publishers of Spurgeon's sermons and other works.

The little book? - *"Morning and Evening Daily Readings"*. It was first published in two separate volumes, one for morning readings and one for evenings. It was so popular that it was then published in one volume. According to one biographer this little volume will "always hold first place". He believed there was more "freshness of thought" in it than in any other of his books. The pages are "full of suggestive through and teaching", many of the readings covering "quite untrodden fields". The German Empress of that time brought a German translation for her personal reading. (see page 62)

Among other first editions I looked at but in my boyhood years but scarcely understood were my grandfather's copy (dated 1879) of *"Eccentric Preachers"*, *"Silver Wedding Testimonial Sermons"* (1879), his hanging-together-by-a-few-threads copy of Spurgeon's *"The Metropolitan Tabernacle: its History and Work"* (1876) (the inspiration for my own *"History"* in 1962, now in its fourth edition), *"Baptist Confession of Faith,"* with a preface by CHS (1879), *"A Catechism with Proofs,"* compiled by CHS, *"An Anniversary Speech for Dr. Barnardo's Homes"* by CHS, and several single sermons such as *"The Sermon of the Seasons"* (my mother's maiden name inscribed in it, 1905), *"Interceding for Transgressors"* (1877), and *"God the Wonder-Worker"* (1887). Besides printed sermons I have some original sermon notes which CHS took into the pulpit, not as some biographers maintain 'written on the back of old envelopes," but written in Spurgeon's own hand on a sheet of his correspondence notepaper with the address printed on it. I have some from Nightingale Lane, Clapham address and others from "Westwood,", Beulah Hill, Upper Norwood. Besides the sermon notes CHS has also listed the hymn-numbers and tunes to which they were sung. In his characteristic abbreviations such as *"T.E."*, that is *'Tabernacle Evening'*, he has noted the time and place and also gives the date. The text at the top is given with the chapter in Roman numerals and the verse numbers in ordinary figures, e.g.: "Ps. XXXIX. 6.7.8."

Dr. Wilbur M. Smith used to say that only figures can help us "appreciate the quantity of devotional and literary material that flowed from the pen of Charles H. Spurgeon". He proved his point in his Introduction to **The Treasury of Charles H. Spurgeon.** Dr. Smith estimated that "the sheer bulk of the literary productions of Charles Surgeon are equal to twenty-seven volumes of the ninth edition of the **Encyclopaedia Britannica!** Spurgeon's widow estimated that not counting *The Metropolitan Tabernacle Pulpit* "one could list perhaps one hundred and twenty titles of Mr. Spurgeon's writings." Adding tracts and pamphlets the number is more than 200!

Is it any wonder that I, as a small boy, sleeping, doing my school homework, playing and having my Quiet Time as a young Christian in the room in my parents' home that housed so many books by Spurgeon, should later turn to writing Christian literature myself?

I began as a student at Spurgeon's College, writing the occasional article for **The Baptist Times**, being encouraged by the editor, through my college Principal, to send in further contributions. Soon, in my first pastorate, the editor of **The Life of Faith** asked me to write a quarterly front page devotional article. The editor of **The Christian** soon followed suit. I then began contributing to **Christian Herald** and various other religious journals. It was not long before I was contributing to religious magazines in America and Canada.

In my second pastorate I had my first book published, a paperback on "Church Publicity" putting my commercial art training to good use. Then sermon, Bible studies, devotional books and historical works followed. But my main love was writing about Charles Haddon Spurgeon, to whom I owed a great debt of gratitude. It seemed only right to try and repay what I owed by putting the record straight from personal contact with a grandfather who 'sat' under him for more than fourteen years. So many of the biographers of my generation were misrepresenting him through merely researching into previous biographies and interpreting them according to their own doctrinal slant. Others were failing to uphold his stand taken over

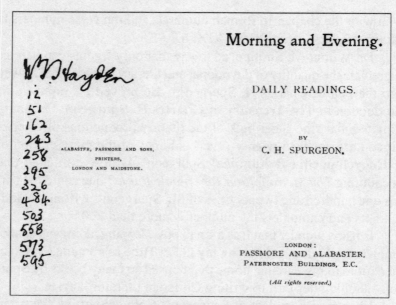

Flyleaf and Title page of my father's **Morning and Evening**.

'mod-ernism' in the Downgrade years. I hope I have managed to give readers on both sides of the Atlantic (and in Hungary and Germany where my books have been translated) a truer picture of Spurgeon's life and ministry, his beliefs and preaching of the doctrines of grace. If so, then it is all due to my early beginnings in that spare room in my parents' home.

CHAPTER TEN

Penmanship ~ Correspondence

Beneath the marble paperweight in my father's den were a collection of postcards and letters in Spurgeon's own hand, plus a few written by Mrs. Spurgeon. Many of my father's books by Spurgeon were bought in London second-hand book shops and these were between the pages as bookmarks! Obviously the readers did not realise how sought-after this correspondence would become in later years. Or may be the original owner of the book died and the relatives selling off the work did not shake them to see if any papers fell out.

There were letters to minister, some well known names, alumni of Spurgeon's College. Others were to members of Spurgeon's college conference. Occasionally there was a postcard from Spurgeon while on holiday on the Isle of Wight (he was fond of Cowes where the yachting is an attraction) or recovering from illness at Menton in the south of France.

Years later when I became a student at Spurgeon's college I made friends with another student who talked of several letters he had regarding the Down-grade controversy. These, he maintained, had never been published and could not while the owner was still living. When he died, some years later, he passed them on to me, and hopefully they will be published one day in America. They do throw light on some of the personalities who were prominent in that sad but necessary controversy. (see page 65)

Soon after his arrival in London his daily correspondence began to assume gigantic proportions. "I was immersed to the chin in letters," he once said. All were handwritten and none was dictated. He believed ink bought in "penny bottles" was as good as any other, and he did not think his letters would be "permanently durable"! The only 'lithographed' (as we would have duplicated followed by photocopied duplicate letters) were the ones sent out in acknowledgment to donors to his various institutions, or to men before a college conference. Even then he frequently added a few lines of his own handwriting. He was as grateful for a child's contribution of a few pennies as he was of an adult well-wisher's generous cheque.

The scope of his correspondence is clear from the Index to his *"Autobiography"*: letters were written to old orphanage scholars, former college students, missionaries, notable brother ministers (e.gs: Dr. Alexander, Archbishop Benson, Bishop Ryle, Canon Wilberforce etc.) members of the aristocracy and of Parliament, Prime Ministers, Florence Nightingale, John Ruskin, The Earl of Shaftesbury, Sankey and Moody, his Tabernacle elders and deacons, and many more.

Sometimes when recuperating at Menton he had to beseech friends through *The Sword and the Trowel* not to bother him and add to the strain he was living under by not writing letters to him. He would sometimes write an omnibus letter in the magazine, or at the end of a published sermon, giving an update on his general health and requesting prayer for some specific need connected with his various institutions.

He once said that a man's autobiography should be written "from the subject's desk" but only so long as at that desk he had not written for the general public. Spurgeon rarely wrote for the general public but his more intimate letters to people have not been collected together in one place. His *"Autobiography"* certainly includes a large quantity of unpublished letters and his son Charles gathered together an important collection in his book *The Letters of Charles Haddon*

not to be
printer
C.H.

Westwood
Beulah Hill
Upper Norwood
1888 Aug

Dear Mr Stockwell,

Pray don't take the slightest notice of the *Mag*. For me to write wd not do you any good but very much the reverse. How cd I help you by denying what is so palpably false? No. I shd seem to countenance these wretched people if I were to deny their rubbish. So on, & mind them not.

Yours heartily
C.H. Spurgeon

Letter from C. H. Spurgeon

Spurgeon. That volume also included as a frontispiece a fine portrait of a young Spurgeon writing with quill pen at his correspondence desk (see page 67).

"A man's private letters often let you into the secrets of his heart", said Spurgeon, and even a cursory reading of Spurgeon's correspondence reveals that his was penmanship that emanated from his heart. He had "the pen of a ready writer" almost copperplate in his early years, but gradually becoming less so with illness and severe pain. Nevertheless it remained neat and clear.

It was time-consuming work. He once said, "Here is another whole morning gone, and nothing but letters! letters! letters!"

How different in the ministry today. As a teenager I turned over the pages of son Charles' book, coyly copying CHS's signature, then trying to make "E. W. Hayden" look something like it! In the ministry I soon found it was quicker to type my correspondence than to use longhand. Nowadays it is not only quicker to use the telephone but the roaring price of postage stamps means that 'phoning is cheaper as well. Like Spurgeon I have always been conscientious with children's mail. I have tried to keep up a regular correspondence with children converted under my ministry, realising they were but babes in Christ and needed regular encouragement if they were to "follow on to know the Lord" and "grow up into Him in all things". It has been a privilege to have them share things with me that perhaps they could not talk about to their parents, especially if they came from a non-Christian home.

One of life's surprises to me was when my parents died and I discovered when clearing up their personal effects, they had kept the letter I wrote to them telling them I had become a Christian at the age of twelve. I have similar letters from child converts in my possession and really how precious they are. Just as precious are the few remaining letters I have in my possession written by Charles Haddon Spurgeon.

Spurgeon writing a letter.

*I*n a memorable service at the Tabernacle every heart was thrilled when Mr.. Spurgeon proposed that the whole assembly should join hands, and form an unbroken chain extending from the floor to the platform, and from the platform to the galleries, and that the congregation should sing.

At first the people were slow to respond, and there was some difficulty about joining of hands of those above and those below; some had to stand on the stairs, but Mr. Spurgeon uttered a cherry word and the thing was done without mishap. There were few dry eyes that evening when the singing had reached the last verse:-

Then in a nobler, sweeter song,
I'll sing Thy power to save,
When this poor lisping, stammering tongue,
Lies silent in the grave.

In the years which have followed, what numbers of that throng have met where they still sing the new song:- *"Unto Him that loved us, and washed us from sins in His own blood."*

~ C. H. Spurgeon Anecdotes

CHAPTER ELEVEN

The Palm Branch ~ Death and Burial

One of the first things I did when I entered Spurgeon's College at the end of the Second World War was to visit Spurgeon's tomb. I was only a short bus ride from South Norwood Hill, where the college is situated, to Norwood cemetery, where Spurgeon was buried.

I expected the cemetery ground to be untidy after six year of being unattended properly during wartime. But I did not expect to see so much bomb damage. All around Spurgeon's tomb the graves of his elders, deacons and Tabernacle members had been scattered. Then I saw the grave I had come to see! The imposing tomb I had been told about by my father and grandfather, the structure I had read about and seen photographs of in the various biographies, was also suffering from enemy air attack. The 'Bible' had been blown from its position above the door and the door was almost off its hinges (see page 70) Both 'Bible' and door were badly damaged. The marble Bible was chipped and the granite door needed repair work to the hinges and lock.

Putting my head inside I saw the coffin of CHS with its palm branch. No, I did not take a leaf of it as a souvenir, that would have

Spurgeon's bomb-damaged tomb in Norwood Cemetery.
Note the open door and the open Bible that has fallen from its cushion.
Up the steps is debris from surrounding graves, some of them being those
of Tabernacle members.

been sacrilege. But I did realise that I was looking at a sight no-one had seen since 1892 when Spurgeon was laid to rest. In 1903 the undertaker and his men might have seen inside when they laid the coffin of Mrs. Spurgeon alongside her husband. So I had that privilege as well; I saw the two coffins.

Withdrawing respectfully, hardly understanding what I had seen, I took a photograph to show the powers-that-be the damage that needed repairing. That photograph was my souvenir.

It was on 31 January 1892 that Spurgeon died at Menton in France. He had preached his last sermon in the Tabernacle on 7 June, 1891. The news of his death flashed around the world. All the world's newspapers carried the headline "Death of Spurgeon", and it was difficult to buy a newspaper as the demand for them was so great.

He was brought back to England in a lead-lined coffin and lay in state in the Tabernacle after it had first been taken to his beloved college the previous afternoon. At night it was removed to the Tabernacle so that his members and a multitude who loved him might pay their respects.

Four memorial services had to be held at which Ira Sankey sang. On the day of the funeral a crowd five miles long, from the Tabernacle to Norwood Cemetery, stood dressed in mourning. The shops were closed and the Orphanage children sat on a raised platform to see him as his coffin passed by. A palm branch was placed on the coffin and his conversion was also there, a Bible open at Isaiah 45:22 - "Look unto me and be ye saved, all the ends of the earth, for I am God and there is none else."

Just before he died at Menton he had stipulated the he only wanted a "plain slab with CHS upon it; nothing more". For the first time ever his elders, deacons and loved ones must have gone against his wishes, even though they had called him "The Gov'nor" for so many years. It was surely love that denied him his last request. A lovely thing was noticed as his body was placed in the tomb - a dove circled overhead, having flown from the direction of the Tabernacle.

He had originally wanted to be buried in the grounds of the Stockwell Orphanage. People would have come to see his grave and would have been prompted to support the orphans he loved so much.

Extension plans for the South London Electric Railway made this impossible, so he choose Norwood Cemetery where already many of his church members had been laid to rest.

I'm sorry his resting place was desecrated by enemy bombs for he himself was a great lover of peace and also a peace-maker. However, I am glad I went to see the tomb the time I did, and was able to report back to the college principal the damage I had seen. He immediately put repair work in hand. To have seen the palm branch in the tomb, an emblem chosen by Mrs. Spurgeon herself, rather than any other wreath as a sign that her beloved was gaining a victorious entrance into the presence of the King. "Blessed is he that cometh in the name of the Lord."

As the dove flew off again, it was noticed that a robin red-breast sang while perched on a nearby tomb. Again how appropriate. Tradition has it that the robin gained its red coat while plucking a thorn from the Saviour's crimson brow at Calvary. They were laying to rest one who preached "Christ and Him crucified" and whose favourite hymn quotation was:

"Dear dying Lamb, Thy precious blood
Shall never lose its power
Till all the ransomed Church of God,
Be saved to sin no more."

And in many an autograph album he wrote the next verse:

"E'er since by faith I saw the stream
Thy flowing wounds supply,
Redeeming love has been my theme,
And shall be till I die."

He continues to preach that redeeming love after his death to the many who visit Norwood Cemetery for those words are engraved along the outside of the tomb in which his earthly remains rest, amidst the dried remains of the palm branch.

CHAPTER TWELVE

A Peculiar Medal – Menton

As soon as Spurgeon died the Spurgeonalia (one is almost tempted to say 'Spurgeon-mania'!) began. Biographies appeared on the book market at frequent intervals, and continued on both sides of the Atlantic for several years. Busts or statuettes of CHS, portraits on mock canvas in the style of oil paintings, etchings, photographs, mugs with a Spurgeon caricatured face after the style of those of John Wesley, all these and many other memorabilia were snapped up by admirers of Spurgeon. Ministers' studies and church vestries had bookshelves or mantelpieces that were graced with some form of Spurgeon memento.

It was not until I became pastor of the Metropolitan Tabernacle that I saw a Spurgeon medal (see page 74); and I have never seen another one. A coin and medal collector sent it to me with the request for information. He did not know who Spurgeon was but found the name of the Tabernacle in a telephone directory. It was the size of an English five pence decimal coin (23 mm in diameter) and had been minted in brass soon after the preacher's death. It was peculiar in the sense that Menton is misspelt: "Mintone". Various biographers could never make up their minds whether to include the final

Both sides of a rare medal. Note mis-spelling of Menton. Photograph by the author.

"e" or not, and indeed some of them use both spellings in the same volume! Some modern, twentieth century, biographers have fallen into the same trap.

A modern world atlas or an up-to-date map of France will show the reader that it is MENTON (see photo-montage on page 76)

Menton was renowned for its beautiful views and warm climate, situated on the French-Italian border of the Cote d'Azur. Spurgeon's sovereign, Queen Victoria, would often retire there during the cold damp winters. His beard not protecting him from the London fogs, Spurgeon also sought warmer climes in the winter, especially when absence from his pulpit because of illness meant a necessary time of recuperation.

He stayed at the Hotel Beau Rivage, well-apportioned for a hotel built in 1876. For almost twenty years Spurgeon visited this sunniest spot on the Riviera. Other like-minded people stayed at the same hotel and what began as family devotions soon became a regular service. Other guests besides those invited to the service began to clamour for an invitation, some even from other hotels. The manager of the Beau Rivage soon had a bell rung for evening prayers and every Sunday afternoon a communion service was held in the preacher's private sitting room, sometimes overflowing into an adjoining apartment. *Till He Come* was eventually published, a collection of his Menton communion meditations.

Among the Christian circle of friends who used to meet with Spurgeon in his hotel were an inner circle of three, the "King's mighty men" as Dr. Wayne A. Detzler calls them. Spurgeon named them when writing his "Personal Notes" in *The Sword and the Trowel* for April 1879: George Muller, John Bost and Hudson Taylor. The first was Spurgeon's hero and from whom he drew inspiration for his Orphanage. The last was the Founder of the China Inland Mission. But who was John Bost? Spurgeon explained in the next month's magazine in an article which he entitled, "Interviews with three of the King's Captains".

Muller he described as "more the idea of Enoch than any man we have ever met; he habitually walks with God." He was amazed at the way he trusted God daily to feed the mouths of 2,050 orphan

A morning walk at Menton.
Photo-montage by the Author.

children. Taylor he described as "lame in gait, and little in stature - but in his spiritual manhood of noble proportions". He so much admired his missionary enterprise that he said, "no other missionary enterprise is so completely to our mind as the China Inland Mission".

Pastor John Bost was the founder of the Asylums of La Force. John was born at the outset of a spiritual revival sparked off by the Haldane Brothers in Geneva, which so affected his father, Ami Bost, that he spent his life proclaiming the Gospel in Switzerland. John began as an evangelist in Ireland. He then studied theology in France and undertook pastoral charge at La Force in the Dordogne. He established homes for epileptic sufferers, the handicapped and the elderly.

He appealed to Spurgeon because he had the same sense of humour. He was large of build and large hearted. At the time of Spurgeon's writing John Bost had founded eight institutions, 366 inmates in all. Spurgeon likened him to Martin Luther - "full of emotion and mental changes, borne aloft to heaven at one time and anon sinking in the deeps." Even while 'resting' at Menton he was lecturing on behalf of his institutions. Spurgeon was "knit to him in brotherly affection."

While Spurgeon very rarely preached series of sermons at the Tabernacle, believing that to publish the titles of a series often restricted the Holy Spirit's influence upon a preacher, he did go through the Gospel of Matthew, verse by verse, at morning prayers in the Hotel Beau Rivage. In his magazine he wrote: "They will, in all probability, come to the public through the press". They were in fact, published posthumously under the title *The Gospel of the Kingdom.*

As a schoolboy of seventeen, waiting to take "A-level" French, I went to France and stayed with a French family for six weeks to teach the children English. My only means of transport was a cycle. I had no money spare for long train journeys. Thus it has always been my regret that I was unable to make the trip to Menton. Having gazed at photographs, drawings, Tom Spurgeon's paintings, in the books in my father's den, biographies of Spurgeon describing his visits to Menton, I should have liked to see it for myself. I often went there in imagination, ringing the bell of the Hotel Beau Rivage and asking to see the visitor's book to see the names Spurgeon and those of the "King's Captains" or "mighty men". Even the peculiar medal I was not able to keep, for economic reasons, but have had to make do over the years with my photographic reproduction. In spite of the misspelling of "Menton" it as kept the biographical mentions of that place alive in my imagination.

CHAPTER THIRTEEN

The Platform Party ~ A Portrait

I n my first pastorate I had a very high platform to speak from in the Sunday school hall where the midweek Bible school (as it was called in those days) was held. I soon discovered the reason why I was so high and lifted up - there were sliding doors each side of the platform and underneath was a vast cupboard.

One day I decided to explore. Sliding back the doors and shining a torch I saw the usual gathered junk that accumulates in such places: old table tennis nets, and bats with the rubber facing pealing off or perished, moth-eaten 'black out' curtains from the days of wartime, trestles (for festive boards) with hinges broken and then ...! Right at the back was an old picture in a badly chipped gilt frame. Dusting it down I discovered an oil painting of C. H. Spurgeon, one that I had never come across before.

The deacons said that I could have it and so I removed the old frame, made a new oak one, varnished the painting, and it hung in my manse studies for many, many years, until it got battered beyond belief by a removal firm. (See page 80)

On one occasion Spurgeon sat for a plaster cast to be made of his face so that a bust could be made for the occasion of his Silver

The author's 'platform find'.

Wedding Testimonial. The finished statuette he gave to the Tabernacle for the vestry but he said the plaster casting was an experience he would never repeat, he disliked it so intensely. With the number of photographic portraits and oils that were executed, and remembering the slow exposures necessary in those early days of the camera, it is a wonder that he sat for so many portraits that eventually appeared in his books, and went on sale to the Tabernacle members and general public.

Do any of them really do him justice? Since the exposure in those days was such a long one, no sitter could keep a smile on his or her face for the duration. All Victorian portraits seem to be of very serious looking people. Spurgeon was no exception. Thus, describing her favourite portrait of her husband, Susannah Spurgeon said, "No angel could look half so lovely ... (yet it had) the semblance of one who knew sorrow and suffering." A smile she could not describe, but rather "the sweet humility, the gentle kindness, the mighty faith in God ... the intense love and unfailing devotion to his Master." That is how she described the finger-pointing-people-to-Christ portrait and also some later ones. Since some may think she was biased, writing as a devoted and loving wife, we must turn to an anonymous biographer ("One who knew him well" was the pen name under which he wrote): "The heavy eyes literally beamed with benevolence when he looked at you. There was a gleam of fun in almost every glance ... in middle life he certainly looked worst, as his portraits plainly show."

From the other side of the Atlantic George C. Lorimer, minister at the Temple, Boston, writing after twenty years acquaintance with CHS said, "The features often described as heavy were lighted by a sunny, limpid smile that seemed to shed over his face a radiance comparable only to the silvery sheen on the bosom of a glassy lake." Flowery language, and in direct contrast to Archbishop Benson who declared, "He is certainly uglier than I had believed!" As a boy turning Spurgeon's portrait to the wall, I would have agreed with the Archbishop.

My "platform 'find' or 'treasure'" I would place way above my father's engraving in the spare room on a scale of one to ten. At least my own children never had to turn him to the wall when they slept in my manse study. But no photographic portrait or one painted in oils has captured the expression described by Mrs. Spurgeon, his anonymous biographer, or the American minister.

While at Menton in 1886 he sat for a further photographic portrait. It was at the request of his publishers, Messrs Passmore and Alabaster. In his "Personal Notes" in *The Sword and the Trowel* he described the resultant portrait as "the best likeness ever taken. The clear light (was) a great help to the photographer, and hence his success." Spurgeon went on to advertise the photographs at one shilling for a "carte" (i.e. post card size) and two shillings for a "cabinet" enlargement (approximately five by seven inches). And they were "post free"!

My own valuable 'find' served as an incentive to preach the doctrines of grace, "contend for the faith once delivered to the saints", support those institutions of Spurgeon that still remained faithful to his principles, and to pray for the continued blessing of his ministry through his sermons and literary works being reprinted and published in this twentieth century.

By looking at his portrait on the wall of my study, so much warmer and more human than the bust or the statuette, I was encouraged in my sermon preparation and my pastoral visitation. His "likeness", as he referred to any portrait of himself, helped me to bear the reproaches and false accusations of fellow-Christians, and also survive the disappointments and discouragements that every pastor is heir to, and to realise the value of encouraging other young men to preach the unsearchable riches of Christ. Whether smiling or serious, benevolent, radiant or severe, it did not matter what others' opinion of the portrait was, for me it was the epitome of a man wholly dedicated to God, whose service was his delight, and in spite of calumny and controversy kept on faithfully preaching for souls, caring for the needy (the orphan and the elderly), and edifying the saints.

Looking back I am glad that in my first pastorate, difficult as it often was, God was pleased to save souls, call young men and women into the ministry and to service overseas, but also led me to look beneath a platform and find such a treasure as a portrait in oils of Charles Haddon Spurgeon.

CHAPTER FOURTEEN

The Pilgrimage ~ Susannah Spurgeon

A mong my souvenirs is a relic of a sad occasion that took place eleven years after Spurgeon's death. On 22 October, 1903, his widow, Susannah, died and four days afterwards was laid beside her beloved "Tirshatha" (her sweetheart name for him) in Norwood Cemetery.

My service leaflet of that occasion tells me that she was not buried from the Tabernacle but the funeral service was held at Chatsworth Road Chapel, West Norwood, before the interrment at Norwood Cemetery.

On the front of the leaflet she is not put as "Mrs. Susannah Spurgeon" but "Mrs. C. H. Spurgeon". Two hymn lines are quoted beneath the time and the place:

"Heaven's morning dawns,
And earth's vain shadows flee!"

On the back of the order of service is the text "With Christ which is FAR BETTER".

The service was conducted by two "Spurgeon's men" - Pastors C. B. Sawday and Archibald G. Brown. It was a simple service with three hymns, a Scripture reading, prayer, address and benediction. The hymns were "Begone, unbelief, my Saviour is near"; "Behold, O Lord, my days are made a handbreath at the most"; and "Sleep on, beloved, sleep, and take thy rest."

I expect not many people kept this paper leaflet. Those who did probably did not think to pass it on to son or daughter who might enter full time service either at home or abroad.

The biographers of C. H. Spurgeon published some years after the preacher's death have little to say about Susannah, except to record her death. Fullerton's (1920), nothing about her life after she became a widow. Carlile (1933) - the same omission. Murray's "The Forgotten Spurgeon" also forgets Susannah Spurgeon (1966). Bacon (1967) nothing. Dallimore (1984) - again nothing about her later life and the finish of her earthly race. So it is like a breath of fresh air to find that R. E. Day in *The Shadow of the Broad Brim* acknowledges that "this exotic British Deborah has had no scribe to give the world her full-length portrait". He goes on to promise that her life, which is "a veritable Eldorado", will be fully dealt with by himself "if the sands of the glass fail not." He desires to write about "her radiant story in *Susannah of Westwood*". Day, an American, published his biography of CHS in 1934, just one year after Carlile's biography.

Susannah was truly a remarkable woman, in her own right as well as being the preacher's helpmeet. It thus seems strange that a month after her passing Charles Ray should have written a book about her life and work and merely ended with the statement: "Mrs. Spurgeon passed away peacefully ... she was buried at Norwood Cemetery in the grave where her husband's remains lay ..." but no mention as to why the funeral service took place at Chatsworth and not at the Tabernacle. A well-written life is marred by such a lack of detail as to her end.

Her life with C. H. Spurgeon began in his New Park Street Chapel days when she had got over her first impressions of his country yokel look and he gave her a copy of Bunyan's *Pilgrim's Progress* on being told that she was concerned about her spiritual life. He wrote on the fly leaf "a blessed pilgrimage". Some time later he gave her a complete set of John Calvin's works!

Interest in spiritual things soon turned to physical attraction when they attended the opening of the Crystal Palace together in June 1854. Spurgeon read her a love poem and asked her whether she ever prayed about who was to be her husband. Baptised by Spurgeon on 1 February 1855 they were married the next year, 8 January 1856.

At first she threw herself most heartily into the work of the church until the birth of the twins Tom and Charles, and then the breakdown of her health after twelve years of happy married life. For sixteen years she was a virtual invalid, hardly leaving her sick room. On one occasion she was operated on by Sir J. Y. Simpson, the celebrated surgeon and discoverer of chloroform. He took no fee for his services.

London smoke and smog affected her health and so they moved to the higher situation of "Westwood", Beulah Hill, Norwood. There they remained until their deaths.

Gifted in personal work Susannah was a spiritual counsellor to many girls and women. She also helped with the administration of believer's baptism, helping the women candidates into and out from the water. She travelled with her husband on his preaching and sight-seeing trips around Europe, often privileged to be in royal company when he preached before the crowned heads of Europe. She laid the foundation stone of the Pastors' College but after that had to rely on letters and her husband's return home from preaching trips, holidays for recuperation in Menton, and other engagements. When he came home exhausted, she would read to him from the Puritans. She helped him with his literary work, proof reading, selecting the texts for the "Almanack" and much more besides.

Then she started her famous Book Fund, sending copies of her husband's work to thousands of poor ministers who could not afford to buy them new. Soon a special room was fitted up for her in the manse and it become a sort of postal and shipping department. During the next twenty years it is estimated that she sent over two hundred thousand books to needy ministers of the gospel. She herself wrote *Ten Years of my Life* and *Ten Years After*, both describing the work of the Book Fund. She also wrote regular "Westwood Papers" and contributed to *The Sword and the Trowel*. After her husband's death she continued his monthly "Notes" in the magazine, writing her own notes and giving encouraging reports of blessing she had heard of through her late husband's printed sermons.

At long last her health improved and she was able to accompany her husband once again when he visited Menton. Her first visit to that lovely place was also her last. Having enjoyed for a short while her husband showing her the sights that she had previously only read about, within weeks she returned home without him at her side. He lay in his coffin.

Her widowhood lasted for a period of almost twelve years, but they were her busiest. She kept on her Book Fund and also worked with her husband's secretary on Spurgeon's *Autobiography*, compiled from his diary, letters and other records.

In 1895, while "Westwood" was being redecorated, she went to live in Bexhill-on-Sea. There being no Baptist Church there she immediately began to establish one. In 1897 she laid the foundation stone.

Susannah was energetic in raising money for the second Tabernacle when the first was burned down. At a reception in the undamaged basement premises she received £6,367 from those attending. With that in mind, and the fact that her son Tom was Pastor of the Tabernacle when she died in 1903 it is strange that she was not buried from her late husband's famous London church.

While we await a definitive life of this great and gracious lady, "bowstring" of a faithful and famous husband, I am glad that I have such a rare souvenir as her funeral service order of service. She was indeed the "pilgrim" Spurgeon prayed she would be when he gave her a copy of Bunyan's class, *Pilgrim's Progress*. In John Bunyan's book, in Part II, the author tells how Christian's wife, Christiana, sets out on the same pilgrimage as her husband and reaches the same destination, the Celestial City. Susannah was Tirshatha's Christiana and on 22 October, 1903 she joined him in the eternal city, her earthly pilgrimage ended.

CHAPTER FIFTEEN
Postlude ~ My Father

I would have few souvenirs of Spurgeon if it had not been for my father. He kept those his father passed down to him, and added to their number as opportunity arose. These he handed down to me, although I had already benefited from them while I lived under his roof.

The day came, when my mother died, that he later came under my roof. I was then pastor of Spurgeon's Tabernacle and he thought it right to join in membership there. It was a great privilege to receive him into fellowship with a handshake at the communion table.

For forty-five years he had been treasurer of a Baptist Church in St. Albans and for the same period of time a local preacher among the Hertfordshire village chapels. In London he continued to preach, but as a popular and welcome speaker at women's meetings, especially those in the five mission stations attached to the Tabernacle. No longer were his preaching engagements on foot, by cycle, along the country lanes of Hertforsdhire. Now he went by bus or underground. And what a change of scenery!

Since so many books and records were lost during the bombing that devastated the Tabernacle during World War II it fell to my lot through the religious press and by other means to make up the deficiency. Gradually I managed to build up a complete set of *The Metropolitan Tabernacle Pulpit* and *The Sword and the Trowel*. I had the damaged oil paintings of Spurgeon' predecessors, Drs. Rippon and Gill, and other worthies, and his own portraits, repaired and re-varnished. A Heritage Room was started, housing Drs R. & G's vestry chairs, Spurgeon's bust and many other Spurgeon memorabilia.

As these objects, books, papers, scrapbooks, and much else came in, it was my father's delight to peruse them (see page 89) for hours. Since he and my mother were married at the Tabernacle, before moving out to St. Albans, it must have been like coming home, although I'm sure he must have missed the Hertfordshire countryside and the quieter way of life in the country. To return to the hurry and bustle of London streets, although every day for 45 years he had come up to London for his work as an accountant, travelling by train from St. Albans. So it was with his father before him. My grandfather often told me that he was 'an Essex man' like Spurgeon, and when he moved to London as a young man to find work he so missed the Essex countryside that he would walk through Kennington Park in bare feet, just to feel the grass between his toes!

My father died during my London pastorate, not in my home but on a visit to my late brother's at Broadstairs. Before he went he had begun to suspect that 'things were not right' at the Tabernacle and it greatly grieved him. He had heard all about a previous "Tabernacle Tempest" from my grandfather, and he knew what I would have to go through. I was glad that he was not present when the clouds broke once again, but I do wish he could have seen us settled again in a country chapel, this time not in Hertfordshire but in Herefordshire.

Although my father was not alive to move with us, the souvenirs he had left me went, and once again they were housed in my new study. Sadly my own son died of cancer at an early age so I have no-one to leave my souvenirs to. That brings the wheel full circle to where I explained at the very beginning of this book how I had had to sell many of them to Spurgeon-lovers in America. As some of my friends over there say, "You English buried Spurgeon; we keep him alive!"

Mr. W. T. Hayden, the author's father, studying an album of old photographs sent in for the Tabernacle Heritage Room.

One day there will be no need of souvenirs for we shall meet C. H. Spurgeon face to face. My father often used to say to me, "If you come looking for me in heaven you will find me between the apostle Paul and C. H. Spurgeon." I rather think we shall all be trying to get nearer the throne than that, longing to see the One who died for us, for we shall not only see Him as He is but we shall be like Him.

Preaching about heaven on one occasion Spurgeon quoted the hymn lines at the end of his address:

"Then shall we see, and hear, and know
All we desired or wished below."

That is it. What our finite minds have not grasped down here on earth; what our eyes and ears have not seen and heard, even with the help of tangible souvenirs, **then**, in heaven, we shall see and hear and understand and know. No artifacts will be necessary. All will be revealed in the wonderful light and spiritual understanding of heaven and eternity.

A postlude, according to a Dictionary of Music is "anything played as an after piece to anything else." While I have entitled this final chapter "Postlude" and made references to my earthly father; the final postlude is when we enter the presence of our Heavenly Father and hear the music of heaven, the voices of our loved ones who have preceded us and are joined with those of the angels and other spiritual beings who are praising the Lamb upon the throne.

CHAPTER SIXTEEN

Postscript – Spurgeon's First and Last Words in the Tabernacle

C. H. SPURGEON'S
First Words
at the Tabernacle

I WOULD PROPOSE THAT THE SUBJECT OF THE MINISTRY IN THIS HOUSE, AS LONG AS THIS PLATFORM SHALL STAND, & AS LONG AS THIS HOUSE SHALL BE FREQUENTED BY WORSHIPPERS, SHALL BE THE PERSON OF **JESUS CHRIST**. I AM NEVER ASHAMED TO AVOW MYSELF A CALVINIST; I DO NOT HESITATE TO TAKE THE NAME OF BAPTIST; BUT IF I AM ASKED WHAT IS MY CREED, I REPLY, "IT IS JESUS CHRIST." MY VENERATED PREDECESSOR, DR. GILL, HAS LEFT A BODY OF DIVINITY, ADMIRABLE & EXCELLENT IN ITS WAY; BUT THE BODY OF DIVINITY TO WHICH I WOULD PIN & BIND MYSELF FOR EVER, GOD HELPING ME, IS NOT HIS SYSTEM, OR ANY OTHER HUMAN TREATISE; BUT CHRIST JESUS, WHO IS THE SUM & SUBSTANCE OF THE GOSPEL, WHO IS IN HIMSELF ALL THEOLOGY, THE INCARNATION OF EVERY PRECIOUS TRUTH, THE ALL-GLORIOUS PERSONAL EMBODIMENT OF THE WAY, THE TRUTH, & THE LIFE.

Spurgeon's first and last words in the Tabernacle published on a double-sided card after his death and one of them bought by the Author's grandfather.

C. H. SPURGEON'S
Last Words
at the Tabernacle

If you wear the livery of Christ, you will find Him so meek and lowly of heart that you will find rest unto your souls. He is the most magnanimous of captains. There never was His like among the choicest of princes He is always to be found in the thickest part of the battle. When the wind blows cold He always takes the bleak side of the hill. The heaviest end of the cross lies ever on His shoulders. If He bids us carry a burden, He carries it also. If there is anything that is gracious, generous, kind, and tender, yea lavish and superabundant in love, you always find it in Him. His service is life, peace, Joy. Oh, that you would enter on it at once! God help you to enlist under the banner of JESUS CHRIST!

Biographical Highlights
of
Charles Haddon Spurgeon

Born in Kelvedon, Essex, 19 June, 1834

Family moves to Colchester, 18 April, 1835

Lives with grandparents at Stambourne, August 1835 to
August 1841

School at New Market, August 1849

Converted in Artillery Street Primitive Methodist Chapel,
6 January, 1850

Baptised 3 May, 1850

Enters Leedings School, Cambridge, 20 June, 1850

Joins St. Andrews Street Baptist Church, Cambridge,
2 October, 1850

Preaches first sermon at Teversham, Spring 1851

First sermon at Waterbeach, October, 1851

Invitation to preach at New Park Street Baptist Church, London,
November 1853

First sermon in new Park Street, 18 December, 1853

Accepted invitation to pastorate, 28 April, 1854

Preached in Exeter Hall, the Strand, February to March 1855

New Park Street Pulpit (printed sermons) first issued January 1855

Married to Susannah Thompson, 8 January, 1856

Twin sons born, 20 September, 1856

Surrey Gardens Music Hall tragedy, October 1856

Sunday morning services held in Music Hall, November 1856
to December 1859

Preached at Crystal palace, 7 October, 1857

Moves to house in New Kent Road, Autumn 1857

Site for Metropolitan Tabernacle bought, 13 December, 1858

Foundation-stone of Tabernacle laid, 16 August, 1859

First meeting in Tabernacle, 21 August, 1860

Tabernacle opened, 18 March, 1861

The Metropolitan Tabernacle Pulpit (printed sermons)
begins December 1861

First issue of *The Sword and the Trowel*, January 1865

Site for Stockwell Orphanage purchased, January, 1867

Preaches in Agricultural Hall, Islington, March-April, 1867

Foundation stone of Orphanage laid, 9 August, 1867

Mrs Spurgeon becomes an invalid in 1868

Helensburgh house built, Summer 1869

Twin sons baptised, 21 September, 1874

Move to Westwood, Beulah Hill, summer 1880

Last sermon preached in Tabernacle, 7 June, 1891

Died at Menton, 31 January, 1892

Buried in Norwood Cemetery, 11 February, 1892

About the Author

Eric Hayden is a former Pastor of Spurgeon's Metropolitan Tabernacle and now lives in retirement in Gloucestershire.

Books by the Author

~ SPURGEON'S LIFE AND MINISTRY ~

A Traveller's Guide to Spurgeon Country
He Won Them for Christ
Highlights in the Life of Spurgeon
History of Spurgeon's Tabernacle
Lectures on Spurgeon
Letting the Lion Loose
Poems and Letters of C. H. Spurgeon
Searchlight on Spurgeon
Spurgeon on Revival
The Spurgeon Family

~ DEVOTIONAL ~

God's Answer for Fear
God's Answer for Pressure
People Like Us

For a full listing of Ambassador Publications write to:

AMBASSADOR PRODUCTIONS LTD.
Providence House,
16 Hillview Avenue,
Belfast, BT5 6JR
Northern Ireland

Emerald House Group Inc.
1 Chick Springs Road, Suite 206
Greenville,
South Carolina 29609
USA